AIR FORCE ACADEMY

Cadets, Training and Equipment

by C. B. COLBY

Coward-McCann, Inc.

New York

Major General William S. Stone, USAF, Superintendent of the United States Air Force Academy. General Stone previously served on faculty of the U. S. Military Academy at West Point, was Commander of Eastern Transport Air Force, Military Air Transport Command, and holds Master of Science Degree in Meteorology and Master's Degree in Economics. His decorations include the Legion of Merit with two oak-leaf clusters, the Bronze Star and Air Medal. His aeronautical ratings include both Command Pilot and Technical Observer.

Contents

All photographs including full-color transparency courtesy of the United States Air Force Academy, Colorado.

United States Air Force Academy

Carved upon the base of a striking statue of an eagle defending its young, presented to the Academy by the Air Training Command in 1958, is this legend: MAN'S FLIGHT THROUGH LIFE IS SUSTAINED BY THE POWER OF HIS KNOWLEDGE.

If this be true, the graduates of our newest service academy should go far indeed, for the education that they acquire below the towering crags of Colorado's Rampart Range is exacting, challenging and strenuous. It is as complete as modern educational science and the ultimate in teaching tools and faculty can make it.

Since the end of World War I, when American airmen realized that the establishment of a service academy for aviation and the science of flight was of paramount importance, dedicated men have been working toward this goal. Not until 1955 when the temporary Academy at Lowry Air Force Base in Denver, Colorado, close to the site of the present Academy, was dedicated, and its doors swung open to America's young airmen-to-be, was this goal achieved. The first graduating class (1959) consisted of 217 men, and when they tossed their caps in the air upon graduation and pinned on their gold bars as Second Lieutenants in the United States Air Force, they launched the traditions of the "Falcons" of our Air Force Academy. In 1958, a year before graduation, the cadets were moved into the Academy complex at its present site.

The Academy is located on 17,900 acres, of which only 10,000 can be used for construction due to the mountainous terrain. The site was chosen from a list of 400 possible sites visited by the committee charged with selection of a proper location. After the close of the Korean War, this committee, appointed by Harold E. Talbott, then Secretary of the Air Force, selected the Colorado site as the most suitable. The altitude of the Academy area ranges from 6,236 feet to 7,100.

The Academy building complex consists of a dining hall, academic building, cadet social center, planetarium, gymnasium, parade and drill field, and athletic fields. The student dormitory and Falcon Stadium, with a seating capacity of 40,000, complete the present complex. Housing for the officers and faculty, a community center, hospital and power plant are also located within the site. All buildings are the most modern constructions of aluminum, steel and glass, with marble used where appropriate. Extensive landscaping adds to the efficient beauty of the Academy grounds.

Main buildings of the complex are named after famous United States Air Force leaders: Vandenberg Hall (cadet dormitory); Harmon Hall (administration building); Mitchell Hall (dining hall); Fairchild Hall (academic building), and Arnold Hall (cadet social center).

The Academy offers a four-year course divided into three basic programs: the Academic Program, the Airmanship Program and the Athletic Program. All programs are designed to accomplish the one goal of the Academy, "to provide instruction, experience and motivation to each cadet so that he will graduate with the knowledge, character and qualities of leadership essential to his progressive development as a career officer in the United States Air Force." Its graduates have already given evidence that the Academy accomplishes this aim.

An average of 800 cadets are accepted each year for the Academy and the stabilized strength of the Cadet Wing is about 2,500. Nominations for appointment to the Academy are open to several different categories of applicants. They include: Congressional (open to residents of the 50 states); District of Columbia and Possessions (open to residents of the District of Columbia, the Canal Zone and the Commonwealth of Puerto Rico); Presidential (open to sons of active, retired or deceased members of the Regular components of the armed forces); Members of the Regular and Reserve Components of the Air Force and Army; Sons of Deceased Veterans; Honor Graduates of Honor Military and Naval Preparatory Schools; and Sons of Congressional Medal of Honor Winners.

An applicant must be at least seventeen years old but must not have passed his twenty-second birthday, and must be a male citizen of the United States. Other qualifications and requirements, both academic and physical, must be met to assure that the candidate will be able to participate successfully in both academic and physical programs and maintain satisfactory marks in both.

Cadets who excel in their studies and athletic proficiency can win any of over forty different types of awards. Those who excel in academic courses are placed on the Dean's List at the end of each fall and spring semester. The cadets who excel in airmanship performance are placed on the Commandant's List, and those who excel in both are eligible for the Superintendent's List. Cadets on the Dean's List may wear a silver star on their uniform sleeve, those on the Commandant's List wear a silver wreath, and those on the Superintendent's List wear a star within a wreath.

Cadets who excel in athletic achievement are awarded individual and team trophies at the Annual Awards Banquet held during June Week. Cadets receive letters and numerals to be worn on athletic jackets for their participation in intercollegiate competition. Special awards are given individual cadets for outstanding achievement in varsity sports.

There are also many opportunities for the cadet to participate in a variety of special activities. These range from work on the staff of cadet publications — Contrails, a book published for the entering class every spring which contains a record of Academy traditions and customs; the Polaris yearbook; The Talon, a monthly cadet magazine, or The Dodo, an informal cadet paper — to serving on any of several cadet committees or forums or taking part in any of several hobby groups.

Already there are many traditions of which the Cadet Wing is proud, and they are most jealous of the Honor Code, administered through elected Honor Representatives of the Wing. This code, "We will not lie, cheat or steal, nor tolerate among us anyone who does," has become a symbol of cadet integrity, and so much a part of the creed of the entire Wing that professors may even leave the classrooms during tests, with complete confidence that the code will never be violated.

On the following pages you will see many phases of cadet life at the Academy, follow a "doolie" through his rugged basic training and accompany the cadets on field trips. You will see something of the Academy and its equipment, see some of its social events and its athletics. I'm sure you will find it as exciting as I did.

Without the enthusiastic cooperation of many at the Academy who worked to help me obtain these outstanding photographs and to provide me with the research material, this book would have been impossible. In particular I would like to express my appreciation to Major James F. Sunderman, USAF, Chief, Magazine and Book Branch, Office of Information, Department of the Air Force, Washington, D. C., and to Captain John M. Connolly, Jr., USAF, Information Officer, Headquarters, United States Air Force Academy, Colorado. To them, sincere thanks.

C. B. COLBY

This fine aerial photo shows the building complex of the United States Air Force Academy in Colorado. The Academy is located just below the Rampart Range and includes nearly 18,000 acres within the boundaries of the property. Many of the buildings shown in this fine photo will be recognized as you turn the pages to follow, and this will give you a good impression of the general layout of the Academy and its grounds.

Academy Chapel and Cadet Dormitory

Designed along strictly modern lines, these two buildings at the Academy serve two important parts of the cadet's program, his religion and his "home life." Top photo shows the unusual chapel, and lower photo shows Vandenberg Hall, the cadet's dormitory. All but First Classmen must attend services; the Fourth Classmen at the chapel, the Second and Third Classes, if they prefer, at churches of their choice in Colorado Springs. In the chapel, Protestant, Catholic, and Jewish services are conducted by chaplains of the different faiths. The chapel features enclosures for all three faiths designed to meet the needs of each. The huge dormitory is designed to give maximum cadet comfort in a minimum of space for sleeping, study and off-duty relaxation. Note ramp leading to lower level, dome of planetarium and rugged mountain range beyond.

Cadet Gymnasium and Falcon Stadium

The athletic and physical education program of the Academy, under Colonel M. L. (Marty) Martin, Director of Athletics, is an extensive and a rugged one. Every phase of the cadet's physical training is aimed at developing strength, endurance, agility and coordination. Top photo shows the splendid gymnasium with its many tennis courts and other outdoor sports areas. Below is an artist's concept of the 40,000-seat Falcon Stadium, built by funds raised through the Air Force Academy Foundation, a group of civic-minded citizens from all over the country. Now let's follow a new "doolie," as the Fourth Classman is called, through the first hectic and exciting days at the Academy, from the last good-bye to his parents (opposite page) until he takes his place as a full-fledged member of the Cadet Wing.

Birth of a "Doolie"

After the cadet has said good-bye to his parents, his transformation from eager civilian into a Fourth Classman begins. First steps include being processed, given required shots, outfitted with uniforms, taught how to march and salute and generally take on the approximate appearance of an airman. As all movements about the Academy are generally in formation, the doolie must be taught to march correctly, salute and move as part of a team rather than as an individual. Top photo shows the doolies dropping their luggage and being directed to the processing line that will lead them through the various steps of entrance. Upperclassmen are in charge of this part of indoctrination. Top photo, opposite page, shows doolies being taught how to stand correctly and assume a military posture. Lower photo shows upperclassmen instructing in proper method of salute. Elementary drill is taught right from start of doolie's life at Academy.

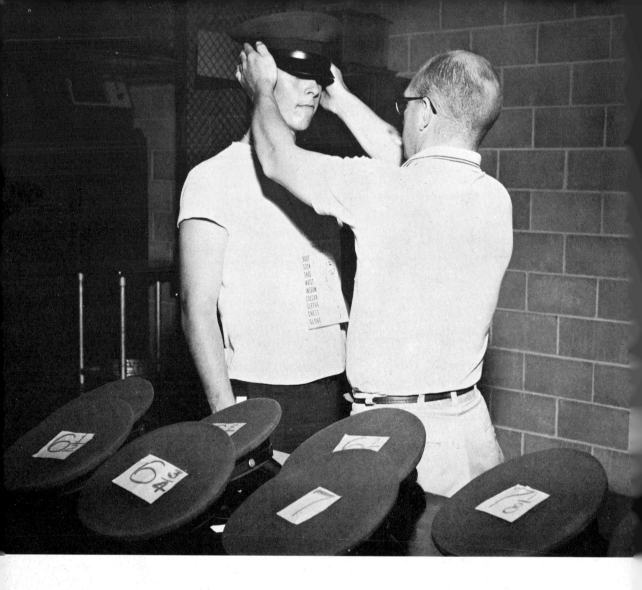

"How's That, Mr. Doolie?"

One of the first steps after the new arrival reaches the Academy is to fit him properly with a uniform. Each cadet starts through the line with a tag attached to his chest with his correct sizes indicated. Here, a fitter checks doolie's hat size, issues a uniform cap and instructs him as to how it should be worn. No cap insignia is worn at this time. Opposite page shows another fitter checking shirt and trousers for proper fit. In the fall of their first year the cadets are issued the distinctive uniforms of the full-fledged cadet, including blue winter dress, two parade dress uniforms (the latter are worn to parades and ceremonies) and accessories. Each cadet must keep his uniforms in spic-and-span condition at all times ready for inspection.

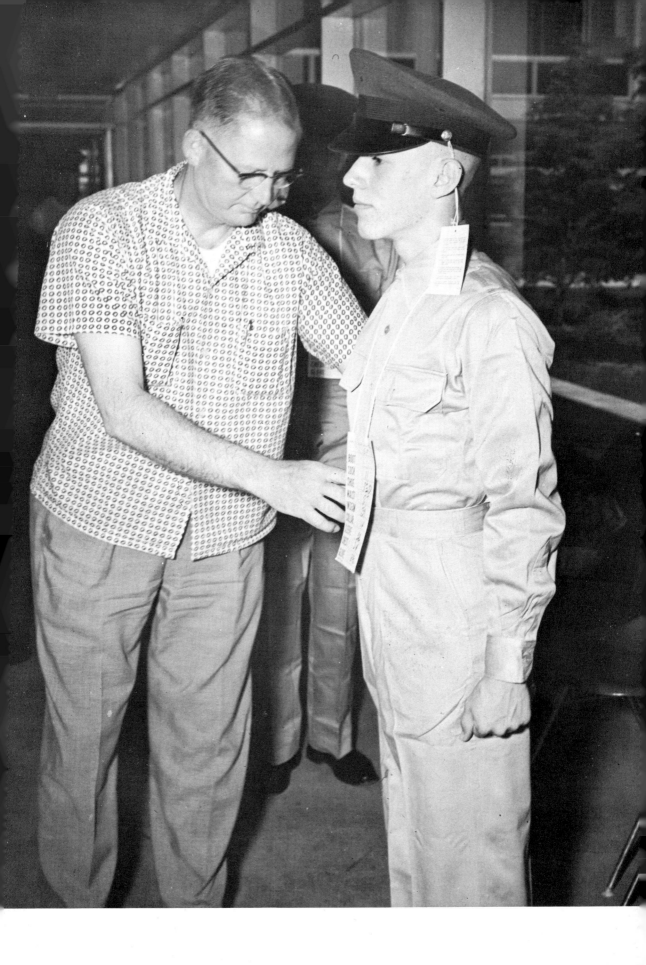

Swearing-In Ceremony

This page shows the new Basic Cadets heading for their rooms after issue of clothing and equipment has been completed. Already they are beginning to feel part of the new life at the Academy. On the opposite page at top is shown a view of the mass swearing-in ceremony late the afternoon of the first day. Those cadets not raising their hands are upperclassmen already members of the cadet body. The Basic Cadets do not wear hats during this important ceremony on the Court of Honor. Lower photo shows all cadets at salute during this ceremony in which new Fourth Classmen become members of the Academy student body. The summer term begins about the end of the first week in June of each year and ends the middle of August. This is the basic term followed by the beginning of the regular fall semester, which starts a few days later.

Close-Order Drill Is a Must

As the cadets march to meals, classes and many other activities, skill and precision in this military art is important to the new cadets. Here an upperclassman instructs the doolies in its fine points. Opposite page at top shows cadets marching to noon meal in vast dining hall where entire student body of about 2,500 cadets is fed at once. Lower photo shows upperclassmen at meal. Every cadet consumes an average of 5,500 calories per day. Typical meal would consist of 200 gallons of soup, 2,000 pounds of beef, 900 pounds of potatoes, 360 pounds of string beans, 120 gallons of salad with 20 gallons of salad dressing, 4,000 hot rolls, 60 pounds of butter, 375 gallons of milk, 80 gallons of coffee and 260 pies. That should be sufficient to keep the cadets healthy and fit in spite of the rugged training they go through, and it is.

A Cadet's Weapons

Skillful use of all types of weapons is important to any military man. The cadets at the Air Force Academy are no exception, and so they are given expert instruction in everything from the manual of arms with the M-1 rifle to skillful use of the .38-caliber revolver, the personal weapon of Air Force crew members. This takes place during the summer training period of the Basic Cadets. This page shows the cadets learning the manual of arms under the supervision of upperclassmen. At the top of opposite page they learn to fire the .38-caliber revolver on one of the ranges. The lower photo shows cadets firing the highly accurate .22-caliber target rifle on the indoor range in the cadet gymnasium. To the left of the cadets are spotting scopes used to check scores and placement of shots. All cadets must excel in marksmanship and knowledge of all weapons which an airman might have to use.

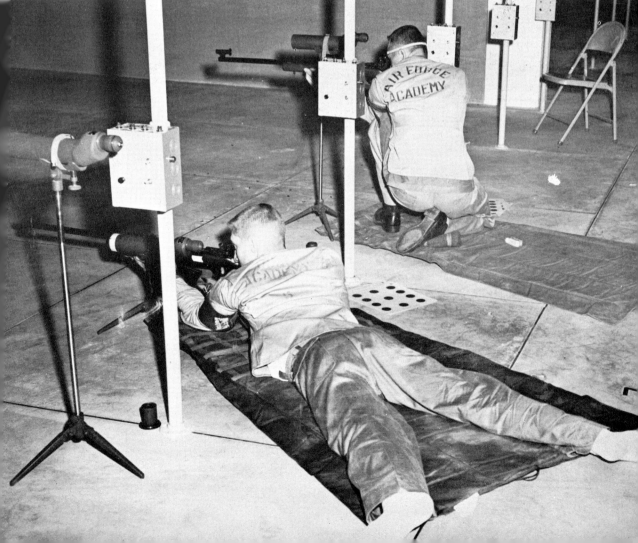

Indoctrination Flights

During the first basic cadet summer training course, the cadets are given indoctrination flights in several types of aircraft. This photo shows a Basic Cadet being fitted with helmet, oxygen mask and parachute preparatory to a flight in a T-33 jet trainer. The mask must fit tightly in order to function perfectly. An intercommmunication microphone is part of the mask and the helmet contains the earphones for two-way conversation between pilot and cadet. Top of opposite page shows cadet and student upon completion of a flight, with another cadet eager for his turn in the T-33 cockpit. Lower photo shows cadet group checking parachutes before entering T-29 navigational training aircraft, where problems in aerial navigation are studied. The flying classroom makes it possible for many cadets to learn firsthand about the intricate requirements for accurate aerial navigation. For many cadets, these orientation flights are their first experiences in the air. Upon graduation, cadets may request flight training at a regular flight training base if they are physically qualified for that branch of the Air Force service.

On the Double!

The first seven weeks of basic training at the Academy put great stress upon the physical fitness of the cadets. Special courses are given to those cadets who require toughening, and all cadets must take part in intramural (competition within the Academy) sports once or twice a week. These include football, soccer, field hockey, cross-country, basketball, boxing, water polo, squash, handball, rugby, swimming, wrestling, judo, and lacrosse, depending upon the season. On the way to the physical training area the cadets (top, this page) move "on the double." Lower photo shows log lifting as part of the special calisthenics training to teach coordination in teamwork. On the opposite page at the top we see some of the Academy gymnasts, and below this, cadets receiving swimming instruction. Physical ability tests are conducted to determine in which athletic area a cadet needs improvement. The first seven basic weeks are tough and toughening.

Heading for a Fall!

The Academy tries to include many carry-over sports in the physical education course; that is, sports which will be of use or pleasure to the cadets after graduation. These include such things as boxing, tennis, handball and others already mentioned. Among those that would be of advantage to every fighting man are unarmed combat and judo, shown here. The instructor at the right is showing how one cadet can use a hip throw to dispose of an opponent.

Obstacle Course

Once the new cadets have been toughened up sufficiently, the physical training program becomes even more rugged, with obstacle courses such as shown above. These are run by the cadets against time and include jumping ditches, climbing walls, swinging on and climbing ropes, scaling log walls and negotiating a wild and weird assortment of obstacles, all designed to test and increase the cadet's endurance and coordination. Some include walking on narrow timbers, for balance, squirming through openings to test agility and skill in awkward physical maneuvers, and some are designed to test courage. Once the doolie has proved his skill and stamina, he is ready for the final "exam," the survival test.

On Their Own

As a climax to the seven-week basic training, when the doolies have been toughened up, they are given a week's training in survival and living off the land. This is carried out in the Pike National Forest, where they learn how to build lean-tos from parachutes, make packs from the chute pack and harness, read maps and use a compass. With a minimum of survival equipment they must live off the land, eating whatever they can catch, snare or otherwise obtain, and then find their way back to the Academy site. Here you see two of the Basic Cadets, studying a map and survival manual in their well-constructed camp. Note the heat reflector of logs behind the fire, the chute used as lean-to roof, and the ground rubbish cleared away from around the fire, a sign of good woodsmanship.

Annual Field Day

Although this looks like a form of mass assault, it's really all in good fun, even though mighty serious in result. This annual Field Day marks the end of the seven weeks of basic training and on this day the cadets vie for honors. The results of the eight events, which include sprint relays, distance run, pentathlon, wall climb, obstacle course, log rolling and tug-of-war, determine which of the training squadrons is the winner. Pushball, shown in the above photo, is another of the events and one which is pretty exciting for everyone. The annual Field Day marks the end of the basic training and now the doolies become Fourth Classmen in an impressive ceremony.

Acceptance Parade

After the annual Field Day, the doolies take part in what for them is a most important event and ceremony. They are accepted into the ranks of the Academy as cadets, rather than Basic Cadets. For the past seven weeks they have been up at 5:30 a.m. and on the jump until 10:15 p.m.; "on the double" (moving at a fast trot) when in the dorm area, and have been subjected to assorted "rules" and orders by the upperclassmen, designed to teach and test self-control, tempers and personality. Not all of this is over, but at least the rugged basic training is behind them. In the impressive Acceptance Parade ceremony they are integrated into the squadrons they will be assigned to for the forthcoming academic year, and become full-fledged members of the Cadet Wing, as the student body is called.

Serious Study Begins

Once the basic training period is over and the fall semester starts, cadets begin their real work in the classrooms. The day of a cadet is a full one, beginning with reveille at 6:25 a.m., after which he dresses and prepares his part of the room for morning inspection. Breakfast is at 7:00 and he has twenty-five minutes to eat it. His classes start at 8:00 and run to 12:00. At 12:20 he marches to the dining hall for lunch but must be back in class at 1:15. Afternoon classes run to 3:15. His afternoons, after class, are spent in drill, command training, study or athletics. Dinner is from 6:30 to 7:00, and at 7:15 he must be in his room studying until taps at 11:00 when, unless he has special permission, he must be in bed with the lights out. It's a tough program for tough young men and, with but few exceptions, they thrive on it. Photo shows one of the language classes in session.

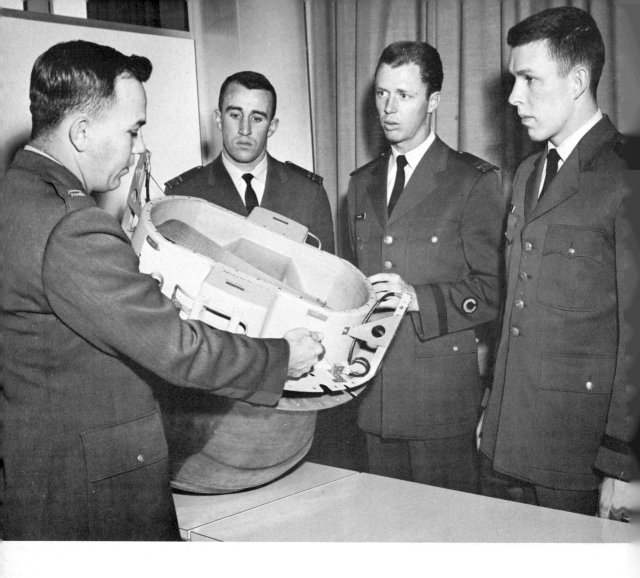

Cadets and Capsule

Naturally, much of the cadet's studies has to do with aeronautics, space travel, and associated subjects. Here a group of cadets and an instructor examine the Discoverer capsule. Mathematics plays an important part in a majority of the technical subjects in the Academy's curriculum, which includes such subjects as physics, mathematics, chemistry, aeronautics, astronautics, mechanics, electrical engineering, English, philosophy, foreign languages and history. In the social sciences, the cadets study geography, cartography (map making and study), economics, political science, psychology and law. Extra courses and activities are available to cadets who keep their marks high enough to permit extra study.

Future Spacemen in Making

In the Department of Astronautics, the cadets study a wide variety of subjects dealing with missiles and satellites, lunar flight trajectories, interplanetary operations, gravity compensation, and many other subjects unheard of just a few short years ago. Here two cadets study the cutaway model of a Titan missile. Many of the cadets now attending the Academy may actually take part in the great adventure of exploring space a few years in the future, so these studies are of prime importance to them.

Tools for Future Space Travel

The technical training equipment of the United States Air Academy includes some of the finest in use today. This photo shows a cadet working out a problem on an analog computer involving the proper placement of a satellite in orbit. In 1958 the Academy established the first undergraduate Department of Astronautics in the nation. Skill in use of such things as computers and a trisonic wind tunnel, as shown on the opposite page, are important to cadets interested in future space travel. The wind tunnel, opposite page, is used for testing wing forms and other astrodynamic shapes up to speeds five times the speed of sound, or roughly nearly 4,000 mph. Lower photo shows the controls with cadets and instructor working on a high speed problem. This is same control panel shown in upper photo with man seated before it. Note students installing test model in chamber of trisonic tunnel.

Academy Library

In Fairchild Hall, the academic building at the Academy, the largest portion of one wing is given over to the library. In this brightly lighted and efficiently planned department, over 130,000 items are available for student use. Eventually the library is expected to contain a quarter of a million items. These are mainly technical reference books, plus some important items, obtained through private donations, regarding the growth and development of the Air Force and the Academy. Over 1,000 magazines and nearly 100 newspapers from all parts of the country, and foreign countries, are to be found here in their current issues, and in a special listening area the cadet may hear foreign languages used in various types of subject matter. There is also a music room. The library is used as a depository for selected United States Government documents as well as some from the United Nations. The microfilm collection includes over 4,500 reels. During one year alone, 67,000 items were circulated, proving the tremendous value of the library to the cadets. Note titles in photo above; opposite, a general view of a portion of the library.

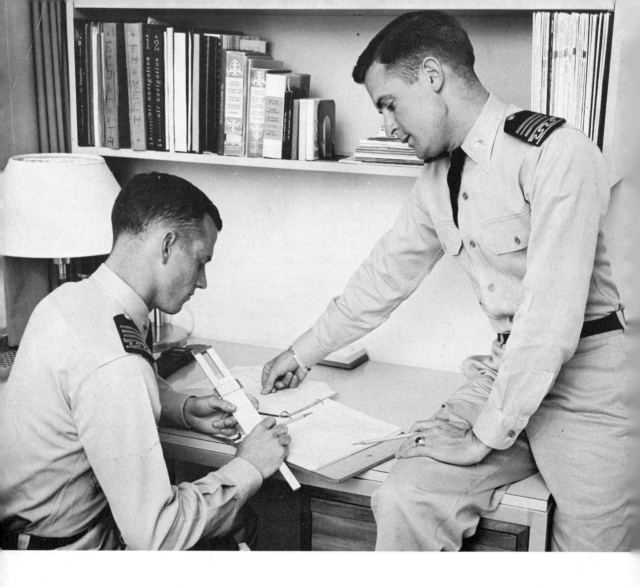

Study and More Study

Study occupies a great deal of the time of every cadet at the Academy. Here we see two upperclassmen working on a math problem in their room in Vandenberg Hall, the cadet dormitory. At the time of graduation each cadet has completed a minimum of 189 semester hours, plus untold hours of serious study to keep up his good marks. The Academy is an accredited institution of higher learning and its faculty is composed of top experts in every subject its academic program includes. The faculty includes about 280 officers, the majority from the United States Air Force, but there are also specialists from the Army, the Navy, the Marine Corps, the Royal Air Force (England), the Royal Canadian Air Force, and even specialists from the air forces of Germany, France, Belgium and Peru. Every state in the Union, and Puerto Rico are represented in the Cadet Wing.

Summer Change of Pace

To gain firsthand knowledge of how the other services operate, summer field trips are included in the Academy program. Here is shown a group of cadets with the Army at Fort Benning, Georgia. Other groups go to Combat Commands and Air Bases in all parts of the country while others travel overseas to visit air bases in Europe, the Far East and Latin America. Some other groups visit missile bases and factories in the United States. Every field trip is designed to make the cadet program more meaningful and to give cadets firsthand opportunity to see foreign as well as United States Armed Forces units in actual operation. The Second Classmen spend a two-week period on individual assignments to Air Force bases with combat squadrons.

Falcons Meet Falcon

Knowledge of our deadly aerial missiles and rockets is important to the overall training of the cadets and, as often as possible, groups are indoctrinated in the construction, maintenance and operation of these weapons. Here a group of cadets is given instruction in the use of the Falcon, one of our air-to-air missiles. This missile is about six feet long and a little over six inches in diameter. It is propelled by solid fuel, and is guided to the target by either radar or a heat-seeking device. The warhead is of conventional explosives. They are carried by fighter planes, to be used against enemy aircraft. Complete knowledge of all our weapons and those of any potential enemy is important to every cadet. On the opposite page another group of cadets is instructed in the art of arming the high-speed machine guns of a fighter aircraft. The individual cartridges of the belt are held together by light metal links which drop off as the piece is fired.

Getting the Feel of Jet Flight

Another summer field trip activity, besides learning about various types of weapons, is demonstration rides in various types of aircraft to give the cadets the feel of jet flight. Many cadets find that this particular phase of Air Force duty appeals to them and they apply for flight training after graduation. Here is shown one of the cadets and Air Defense Command pilot just before a ride in an F-104 Starfighter. This sleek fighter is built by Lockheed, has a top speed of over 1,400 mph, and is armed with the T-171 20-mm cannon, missiles, rockets or nuclear weapons. It has a range of over 1,000 miles and a ceiling of over 91,000 feet. Because of the high mounted elevators on the vertical rudder, the ejection seats discharge the crew downward rather than upward.

Wright-Patterson AFB Briefing

During the summer field trips, known as "Field Study of the Armed Forces," the cadets visit such exciting and educational establishments as Wright-Patterson Air Force Base in Ohio, where the famous Air Force Museum, the Air Force Institute of Technology and Headquarters for the Air Force Logistics Command are located. Here the cadets can find and examine almost every type of aircraft, from the Spad, Camel, Nieuport, etc., of World War I to the latest types, as well as some historical models. In the photo above a civilian expert briefs the cadets, during their visit, on weather satellites and similar space-age gadgets to keep them up-to-date on what America is doing. Note the distinctive "shoulder boards" worn by the cadets with their short-sleeved summer uniforms. The Basic Cadet, or doolie, is not permitted to wear these until he is a member of the Cadet Wing, after the Acceptance Parade and the beginning of the fall semester.

Overseas Instruction

During summer field trips to overseas bases of both USAF units and those of friendly nations, the cadets have opportunities to get to know personnel and equipment at many bases. These trips enable the young men to see how things are done by the "pros," many of whom are veterans of combat service. Above, a veteran mechanic, Master Sergeant Quentin W. Adcock, 417th Tactical Fighter Squadron, at the Headquarters of the 17th Air Force, Ramstein Air Base, Germany, is explaining the J-57 jet engine of an F-100 fighter to two cadets. On opposite page, Academy cadets look over a British RAF jet during European field trip. Note unique ladder designed to fit over jet intake.

Football "Falcons"

Known as the "Falcons," the Academy football team, pictured here in white, although comparatively young, has run up an impressive list of victories. The season consists of about ten games with such opponents as UCLA, Baylor, New Mexico, Maryland, Kansas State, Colorado. All varsity teams, regardless of the sport, are known as the "Falcons" and the intercollegiate teams include such sports as football, cross-country, soccer, basketball, fencing, gymnastics, pistol and rifle shooting, swimming, skiing and wrestling during the fall and winter. Spring intercollegiate sports include baseball, golf, tennis and track. The cadets who participate in these activities must keep up their marks. However, half of the cadets participate in intercollegiate sports each year on a purely voluntary basis, a remarkable record.

Cadet Hobby Clubs

In spite of the hard schedule of academic studies and required sports participation, the cadets have plenty of time for nonscheduled activities. The cadet social center, Arnold Hall, offers many types of activities from bowling to bridge, while out in the wilds of the Rampart Range mountains behind the Academy there is hunting and fishing. There are many clubs for outdoor as well as indoor activities, including the Archery Club (see photo above), Falcon Handlers Club, Fishing Club, Saddle Club, Ski Club, Gun Club, and others. For the cadets who prefer less active hobbies there are clubs for chess, bowling, geography, model engineering, debate, public affairs, the Chorale, and others. Every cadet with a special interest can find someone to share it, but the cadets all enjoy the several big social affairs of the year, particularly the Ring Dance.

Annual Ring Dance

June Week, the exciting and colorful finale of the year for Second Classmen, is capped with the annual Ring Dance held on the evening of the day these cadets, about to enter their final year at the Academy, receive and can wear their treasured class rings. This dance (the cadets receive 10 hours of professional dancing instruction during first year at the Academy) is held in the ballroom of Arnold Hall, where other social events, particularly during the Christmas holiday season, take place. Good manners, social graces and poise are taught the cadets as part of their progress in becoming officers. Above is a general view of the Ring Dance and on the opposite page a trio of cadets and their partners descend the spiral staircase to the dance floor.

Squadron Formation in Formal Review

With the Rampart Range of the Rockies and the Academy buildings behind them as a fittingly rugged backdrop, the Cadet Wing swings across the vast parade ground in formal review. These formal reviews are held every Saturday morning at 11:30 as part of the weekly program. These Cadet Wing parades are equal to those of any of the other services, and the visitors who are welcomed to view these events never fail to thrill to the sight. The entire Cadet Wing takes part in Squadron Formation, and here the training in marching, learned during the first seven weeks of basic training, shows off to best advantage.

"Gentlemen, You Are Dismissed!"

With those words, the last order from the Air Force Academy's Commandant of Cadets, the graduation class tosses their caps high in the air in typical service academy tradition. The new second lieutenants, their cadet days finally over, are now ready to begin their assignments in the regular United States Air Force. Some may go into research, some into administrative work, others may go on to flight training. All, no matter which branch of the Air Force they choose, know that they have proved themselves as cadets, have made the grade and have received the best training for their future careers that America can give them. We can all be proud of these fine young airmen and wish them well as they pin on their gold bars and begin a career in the greatest Air Force in the world.

"Mach I"

As a last page I have selected the mascot of the United States Air Force Academy, the falcon. This bird, chosen because of its strength, alertness, aggressiveness and poise in flight, seems ideal. All falcons, when serving as mascot, bear the name of "Mach I" (speed of sound). This particular bird, named Aethol, is a white gyrfalcon, native to the arctic ice cap of Greenland, where it was captured. There are several falcons at the Academy, trained and handled by the cadets, who show them off in demonstration flights at sporting events. A proud bird, symbolic of a proud Academy.